ETHEREUM: UNDERSTANDING ETHEREUM

ETHEREUM: UNDERSTANDING ETHEREUM

BEGINNERS GUIDE

Charlie Pryce

https://www.amazon.com/dp/B078L7CFXX

© Copyright 2017 - All rights reserved.

You may not reproduce, duplicate or transmit the contents of this book without direct written permission from the author.

You cannot hereby under any circumstance blame the publisher. Nor may you hold him or her to legal responsibility for any reparation, compensations, or monetary loss owing to the information included herein, either directly or indirectly.

Legal Notice:

This book is copyright protected. This is only for personal use. You cannot sell, use, alter, distribute, quote, take excerpts or paraphrase in part or whole the content within this book without obtaining the consent of the author first.

Disclaimer Notice:

Please note the information contained in this document is for educational and entertainment purposes only. We have made every attempt to provide accurate, up to date and reliable information. We do not express or imply assurances of any kind. Readers admit that the author does not attempt to give legal, financial, medical or professional advice. The content of this book has come from various sources. Please consult a licensed professional before attempting any techniques outlined in this book.

By going through this document, the reader comes to an agreement that under no situation is the author answerable for any losses, direct or indirect, which they may incur because of the use of information contained in this article, including, but not restricted to, —mistakes, oversights, or inaccuracies.

Contents

INTRODUCTION 1

CHAPTER ONE: BASICS OF ETHEREUM 3

CHAPTER TWO: FUNCTIONING OF ETHEREUM AND ITS APPLICATIONS 13

CHAPTER THREE: MAKING MONEY 21

CHAPTER FOUR: UNDERSTANDING ETHEREUM 27

CONCLUSION 35

SOURCES 37

Introduction

I want to thank you for choosing this book, '*Ethereum: Understanding Ethereum - Beginners Guide.*'

Cryptocurrencies have made many people rich, while others are regretting not getting into the game in the early days, while even more people are skeptical about the whole thing. All of this started with the launch of Bitcoin and the Blockchain technology that powered it. Now, we have reached a point where Bitcoin's value continues to rise each day, and new cryptocurrencies, as well as blockchain-based applications, continue to appear.

One of these is Ethereum – many have compared it to Bitcoin, and regarding market valuation, it's second only to Bitcoin. Ethereum in its most basic sense is a vast network that is based on a technology known as the blockchain. What Ethereum does is simple – it is an open-source platform and, therefore, it allows people to create decentralized applications on the Ethereum network. Ethereum hasn't just stopped there. It has expanded itself to have its cryptocurrency known as Ether and can be used to carry out smart contracts.

All of this makes Ethereum unique and while Bitcoin is just a cryptocurrency, Ethereum is far more than that because it's not limited to only being a cryptocurrency. So, concerning investment, trading and making money, Ethereum is the new big thing and in this book, you'll be able to learn what Ethereum is, how it works and how you can use it to your benefit.

Thank you once again for choosing this book, hope you find it informative.

Chapter One:
Basics of Ethereum

In the most basic form, Ethereum is a blockchain-based open-source platform that gives developers the opportunity to build decentralized applications and deploy them. Like Bitcoin, it is a distributed blockchain network that is public, but there are some significant differences between the two.

The most significant difference is the purpose and the capability of the two networks. Bitcoin offers a specific blockchain application, that of a P2P digital cash system that allows for online payments of Bitcoin. This network is used to track the ownership of the Bitcoin, but Ethereum is focused on the program code needed to run a decentralized application.

With the Ethereum blockchain, rather than Bitcoin, the miners will work to earn Ether or ETH. Although this is a type of digital currency, rather than being spent in the same way as we can make purchases with Bitcoin, ETH is the fuel that is needed to run the Ethereum network. It can be traded but is used by the application developers to pay for the services and the transaction fees on the Ethereum network.

A Russian Canadian engineer proposed his idea for Ethereum in the year 2013. Vitalik Buterin took what he had learned from working with Bitcoin and decided that he was going to create a blockchain application that would surpass Bitcoin. In 2014, Ethereum was funded and started the development process.

When the developers were working on Ethereum, they decided that they wanted to go beyond the peer-to-peer system and provide more services to users that Bitcoin was not able to offer. But, as Ethereum was being developed, people began to question its security and its scalability. Even now, people are continually questioning the security and scalability of Ethereum.

In the summer of 2015, Ethereum's blockchain went live. In the beginning, Ethereum's programs were being developed by The Ethereum Foundation and the Ethereum Switzerland GmbH. In the spring of 2016, the Ether token was created and held a net worth of one billion dollars. The Vox website reported, "Ethereum is a new digital currency and is a challenge to Bitcoin because of the wide range of services that Bitcoin was unable to offer."

IMPORTANT ASPECTS OF ETHEREUM

In this section, we will look at the fundamental aspects and functions of Ethereum – some of these will be discussed in detail in the later chapters.

Smart Contracts

In a later chapter, I will be showing you how to build a Smart contract but, for now, we are just going to look at what they are and what they can be used for. A Smart contract is a bit of computer code that contains instructions for a transaction or exchange of something of value to take place upon certain conditions being met. They are programmed to run on the blockchain, as these contracts act exactly as they should and execute exactly when they are programmed to do so, without the interference of any third-party and the risk of hacking or downtime.

All blockchains can process code, but most of them are limited in what they can do. That is where Ethereum differs. Instead of developers being curtailed by a limit on operations, they can create the operations they want to use. This means there is the potential for thousands of applications that can go beyond anything ever seen before.

Virtual Machine

Before Ethereum came into existence, blockchain applications could only be designed to do limited things. The cryptocurrencies were designed to do one thing – operate as P2P digital currencies, nothing more. This posed a problem for developers. They either had to expand the range of functions that these cryptocurrencies could do, which would be complicated and take too much time, or they could come up with a new kind of blockchain-based platform and application. The developer of Ethereum, Vitalik Buterin, came up with an innovative approach.

The core innovation of Ethereum is the EVM or Ethereum Virtual Machine. It is a Turing-complete software running on the Ethereum network, enabling anybody to run whatever program they want regardless of what programming language it is written in, given sufficient memory and time. The EVM simplifies the process of creating blockchain-based applications and makes it all more efficient. Rather than needing to build a new blockchain for each application, the EVM enables thousands of different apps to be built on one single platform.

Uses of Ethereum

Ethereum is primarily for developers to build their decentralized applications on and to deploy them. Otherwise known as Dapps, these applications will serve a specific purpose. Bitcoin is a Dapp that provides the P2P digital cash system for example. As these applications are comprised of code that runs on the blockchain, no one person or entity controls them.

Think of all the different intermediary services that are used across all the different industries. From banks to other services that we rarely give a second thought to, like regulatory compliance, voting systems, etc., if the service is centralized, it can easily be decentralized with Ethereum.

Although the decentralized application comes with a ton of benefits, it is not completely without fault. Humans write the code for the Smart contracts, and they are only as good as who writes them. Any oversights, bugs in the code or sheer human error can lead to things happening that weren't meant to and if a mistake is exploited, there is absolutely no efficient way to stop it. The only way would be to get consensus from the network and rewrite the underlying code. This is not what the blockchain is all about because it is meant to be immutable and any action that a central party does will raise questions about the apparent decentralized nature of the application.

There are lots of ways to plug yourself into the Ethereum network, but by far the best and easiest is to use the native Mist browser. Mist is user-friendly and provides you with a digital wallet for storage and trade of ETH tokens – later I will show you how to set up a Mist wallet. Mist also allows you to write smart contracts as well as managing them, deploying them and using them. Like a normal web browser provides access to the net and helps you to navigate it, so Mist is a portal to the decentralized blockchain application world.

You can also use a browser extension called MetaMask. This transforms Google Chrome to an Ethereum browser and lets anyone develop or run a decentralized app from the browser. Although it was first built as a plugin for Chrome, in time it will also provide support for Firefox and other platforms.

It is early days yet but Mist and MetaMask, not to mention other browsers, are starting to give us more access to decentralized applications. Even if you are not of a technical background, you can still build that decentralized application, a revolutionary jump that could bring the Dapp firmly into the mainstream.

We can also use Ethereum to build DAOs – Decentralized Autonomous Organizations. These are decentralized organizations that are fully autonomous, having no one leader. They are run purely by programming code and smart contracts that have been written on Ethereum. This code replaces the structure and the rules of a traditional organization and eliminates the need for centralized control and people. Each DAO is owned by those who purchase ETH tokens but, rather than the tokens acting as equity shares or ownership, they provide the token owner with voting rights instead.

PROS AND CONS

A lot of people do not know that there are more cryptocurrencies than Ethereum and Bitcoin. However, why would you still want to choose Ethereum over any other cryptocurrency? Below, you will see the pros and cons of Ethereum to help you make an informed decision on whether you want to invest in Ethereum now or at some time in the future.

Contracts

Quite often, when a contract is written, a lawyer has to look at it, and a judge has to enforce it. This will be an expensive process. So, Ethereum offered smart contracts as a way to provide a cheaper contract solution. The smart contracts will be governed by the distributed autonomous organization.

Due to the distributed autonomous organization, you are not going to have to worry about how your contract is written or if it will be carried out, as you want it to be. Each contract will be required to work inside of the DAO's rules. This way both parties involved in the contract are protected.

Due to the DAO, there is not going to be any need for judges or lawyers to be involved in your contract process. At the same time, you need to make sure you reread your contract before you send it to the system. A trustless operation system has never been established, but Ethereum is using the way that technology evolves to attempt to create one.

Distributed Autonomous Organization

Digix was funded with five million in ether so that another cryptocurrency called Dapp could be created. This cryptocurrency is backed by gold that makes it different than any other cryptocurrency. Dapp's funding was raised in one day. Thanks to the funding, it was able to start the company right away without having to wait for the financing. Once they started their business, they were able to create a board that determined how tokens would be distributed and various other things that would require someone to make the decision. This took investors, banks and lawyers out of the equation. While investors were left out of the equation is not normal, it does take some stress off them because it is terrifying to invest in a company that doesn't know what will happen to them.

The DAO will take the options that are required for the contract and simplify them into a single layer to help developers and users have an easier time in working on the platform.

Low cost

Since Ethereum works off the DAO, it will eliminate the costs associated with the business functions as they are done automatically. This is mostly because you do not have to purchase an office building. (Details mentioned in the later sections).

EtherEx will provide you with a decentralized system that will have a cryptocurrency in secure and trustless fashion. The EtherEx will work on an infrastructure that is similar to Digix where there will be a group of people who make important decisions. This board and the foundation have assisted in reducing the gas cost for a nonprofit organization.

Ethereum will reduce the cost of setting up when a business is built on a DAO. You are no longer going to need your building or to spend on office supplies. However, there will be a small cost involved for using the DAO, which is not going to be anywhere near to the cost involved in renting your building or buying the office supplies. On top of this, you will have an unlimited number of employees working for you remotely.

Still new

Ethereum is still new, and it will continue to be developed so that their users can hopefully have a platform that can offer them anything they could possibly want. When you compare Ethereum and Bitcoin, you will see that Bitcoin is more established, but it cannot provide what Ethereum can offer.

Legal advice

Ethereum has eliminated the need to involve judges and lawyers in your contracts. This can be good because you will be saving money. But, you have to know how the system works to ensure that you are making a decision that will be the best for you. The only thing you will have to worry about is that computers will have flaws, so a human has to be there to ensure that the platform and its code are running efficiently.

Changes

Since changes come with regular updates, you will have to ensure that your system applies the required updates by shutting down the servers promptly to avoid the servers getting overloaded so that it doesn't shut down without a warning.

Remote employees

Since you will have employees who are not going to be working in the same place you are, you will have to deal with them being in different time zones and even with them being distracted by their personal lives. So, make sure that you understand what is going on with your employees and help them to understand what they will be dealing with as they work for you.

Competition

One of the biggest things that you will have to deal with is competition. There may not be enough competition, but if that happens, then you will be around for a very long time. But, when there are too many people on Ethereum, then you will have a lot of people to fight against when it comes to mining pools.

There will be plenty of good things that will come from using Ethereum just like there will be bad things. Ethereum helps in using technology and evolving to create an entirely new world of digital currency. You never know what will happen with Ethereum as it keeps evolving and you will be part of the history when you decide to use Ethereum.

Chapter Two: Functioning of Ethereum and Its Applications

Ethereum Blockchain

Today, Bitcoin continues to be the largest, open public blockchain and serves as the definitive model upon which many other blockchain-based applications are based. However, the Bitcoin blockchain is only one implementation of blockchain technology. As more and more industries begin to explore the potential of the blockchain, new models are emerging on a regular basis, often suited to serve a specific purpose.

When we look at Bitcoin, we see that fundamentally its purpose is a decentralized, peer-to-peer digital currency. Bitcoin solves a particular problem: how to make secure financial transactions on a peer-to-peer basis from anywhere in the world while eliminating the need for trust, a middleman or centralized authority like a bank. While Bitcoin is not perfect, it has been quite successful in terms of serving the purpose for which it was intended.

As developers and entrepreneurs began to see implications for blockchain technology that went far beyond financial transactions, many began to imagine alternative blockchain structures that might be more suited to accomplish different functions. Vitalik Buterin, the developer who invented Ethereum, envisioned an open platform upon which anybody could build a blockchain-based application to perform any kind of function.

Rather than a blockchain that simply stored financial transaction data, as with Bitcoin, the Ethereum blockchain is designed to execute code based on verified transactions. Instead of simply moving funds from Account A to Account B, as with Bitcoin, Ethereum could create an environment where a transaction from Account A to Account B could trigger a vast range of events. For example, transactions in Ethereum can be used to register a new domain name, transfer property titles, manage voter registration, or execute secure contracts between two or more parties. In fact, "transactions" within Ethereum are often referred to as "smart contracts."

SMART CONTRACTS

The term "Smart Contracts" comes up a lot in reference to Ethereum. What is a smart contract? The short answer is that a smart contract is a computer program. Smart contracts are really the "meat and potatoes" of Ethereum, and it is worth exploring this concept in some depth in order to really grasp the power and vision of the platform.

If you don't have much in the way of a technical background, don't worry. When it comes to actually writing smart contracts, you will need to learn to code or hire a programmer, but you don't need to know how to code in order to understand, conceptually, how smart contracts work. However, it is helpful to have a basic understanding of how computer programs work, even if you don't necessarily know how to write them yourself.

While they can do incredibly complex things, all computer programs essentially work by asking a series of yes or no questions. When we think about all "data" ultimately consisting of 1's and 0's, or binary code, what those 1's and 0's represent are "yes's" and "no's." Broadly speaking, there are no "maybes" for a computer. If we could write a simple computer program in English, it might look something like this:

"Dear computer, if I am playing a video and I click the pause button, then please pause the video."

In this example, the computer will first need to check if I am playing a video. This is the first "yes or no" question it will need to answer. If the answer is "yes," I am playing a video, then it will ask question number two: am I clicking the pause button? Let's say I'm not. For as long as I am playing the video (i.e., as long as the first answer is still "yes"), the computer will wait, patiently, asking that second question over and over again until the answer is "yes." Its only mission in life, as long as I am playing a video, is to check constantly whether or not I am pressing the pause button. As soon as I do press the pause button, the answer to the second question becomes "yes," and then it will pause the video.

When we think about digital transactions happening with Bitcoin, what we're really doing when we participate in these transactions is executing a simple computer program. The essence of what happens is that Person A sends funds to Person B. Bitcoin's software will ask a series of questions: Does Person A actually have sufficient funding? Can Person A verify ownership of the address holding those funds? Is the address for Person B valid? As long as the correct inputs are provided, the decentralized Bitcoin network will reach a consensus for performing the computations and executing the program: the transaction will be verified, and Person B will receive the funds.

With Bitcoin, the program that is running only deals with one type of transaction. "Bitcoins" are essentially just numbers that are moved around from one digital address to another, and the record of all of those moves is stored on the blockchain. The blockchain provides a system for a decentralized network of computers to reach a consensus about which tasks to perform and then to perform said tasks. In the case of Bitcoin, the "tasks" are transfers of the coin from Person A to Person B, but is there any reason why this system couldn't be used to handle other types of tasks? Well, no, and that is precisely what Ethereum is built to do. Ethereum uses the same blockchain infrastructure, but it opens the door for any type of program to be executed.

Even when we continue to think in terms of financial transactions, the possibilities that Ethereum offers allow for things like conditions, creating a much more flexible environment for payment systems. For example, with Ethereum, a secure deposit could be held on the blockchain for a specified period of time. If a set of conditions were not met, it could be returned to the payer; if the conditions were met, the payment could be released to the payee. In Bitcoin, there is no way to hold the payment in "escrow" like this without the use of a third party. This kind of conditional transaction is a simple example of something that could be executed with a smart contract in Ethereum.

As we become more integrated into the Internet of Things, smart contracts open up a whole world of possibilities. For example, as smart cars become more prevalent, we could easily envision a transition from the old system of needing to put money in a parking meter to a system that would run entirely on smart contracts. Sensors could easily link specific cars to specific parking spaces, and a smart contract could be used to automatically deduct the appropriate fee based on the time a car was parked in a given space. Rather than digging around for change under the seat and dealing with parking meters, drivers could just park and the smart contract would manage the transaction in the background. Cities could do away with the entire system of meter maids and automate the entire process.

At the point of exchange, when you buy the toothbrush, a network of smart contracts could immediately inform the warehouse that the store needs more inventory, which would, in turn, inform the manufacturer that they would need to get another shipment ready for the warehouse, which will, in turn, let the plastic supplier know that, in order to make more toothbrushes, the factory in China will need to have more raw materials shipped over to them.

The advantages to automating this entire system via smart contracts include eliminating a huge amount of paperwork, bureaucracy, delay time, human error and fees associated with middlemen required in each instance to physically contact the next link up in the supply chain and negotiate each order. Making these incredibly complex systems more efficient and less vulnerable to corruption by creating a transparent record of every transaction is one of the most promising applications for smart contracts.

THE ETHEREUM VIRTUAL MACHINE (EVM)

A virtual machine was put in place for Ethereum so that security could be taken care of whenever code that cannot be trusted is executed since almost every computer in the world executes this piece of code. Whenever you observe the virtual machine, you will realize that the virtual machine will work on Ethereum's security against attacks; more specifically DOS attacks that are directed at cryptocurrency platforms. The virtual machine is also going to make it to where external programs are not able to interfere with any communication points that are running the program.

The chances are that you are not a programmer, so you are not going to know what a DOS attack is let alone how to prevent one. Therefore, you need to understand what they are and how the virtual machine will stop them from attacking the Ethereum system.

Ethereum virtual machine will run off a runtime environment as smart contracts are executed. And, with how popular smart contracts are becoming by Ethereum users, it is possible that these smart contracts will take over the financial industry. However, the smart contract technology will complete tasks that have to be achieved without having supervision, which makes it a version of machine learning.

A paper written by Dr. Wood stated that the virtual machine was created in a sandbox environment. It means they will have the ability to change the future of cryptocurrency because there is one piece of code that will outperform every other platform.

The sandbox environment is not going to be the ideal environment because you are not going to be able to see the program's full potential because the initial status continuously changes. Sandbox environments are not going to be like the real world because the users will use the program in a way that is different from how a computer will use it. But, testing the program in a sandbox environment is one of the safest ways for the developers to check the constraints of a program without releasing it to the public. This means they can ensure that the coding for the program is right and is not going to crash on the users thus causing the users to get upset and possibly leave the program for good.

While you watch the day to day operations on a decentralized system, you will know that the virtual machine will be what is in charge of making sure those tasks are completed in the order that they are supposed to be completed in. The best thing about the virtual machine is that it's free. This means that any programmer can download it and use it.

CHAPTER THREE:
MAKING MONEY

GETTING ETHER

When it comes to getting Ether, you will need to follow the steps listed below.

1. Create an Ethereum wallet. The wallet that you create will be where all of your Ether will go so that you can send out payments as well as receive them. Sadly, when you look at Ethereum, you will notice that since it is still a new platform, it may be difficult to find online wallets that are user-friendly. Some users will use Ethereum and can testify that ether wallets can be made out of an online wallet generator that will give you public and private keys so that you can access your wallet without anyone else getting into it. My Ether wallet is a program that will enable you to print out your wallet and keep it in a safe place. It is recommended that you download the JSON file and place it in various locations so that you have access to it if something happens. As new transactions are created, your private key will have to be put into the file so that you can show that you are who you say you are.

2. You will need to obtain Ether. You can exchange money for Ether, or you can mine it. When you are buying Ether, you can use shapeshift.io. This is a user-friendly site that will make it easy so that you do not have to register with them. You will have the option of switching between thirty-two different

cryptocurrencies without any problem occurring on your end. But you may find that you have an issue with some of the cryptocurrencies because there are not enough people who use them. So, purchasing them is not going to do anything for you but waste your time and your money. One of the things that you will need to keep in mind is that no matter what cryptocurrency you choose, there will be a deposit box and a receiving box. As you place your public address into Ethereum, you will agree to their terms before clicking start. Now that you have done that, you will get a deposit from the system to make sure that you can send and receive coins. It is only going to take you a few minutes before you see your balance go up in your wallet. When you choose to mine with Ethereum, you must have a GPU card in the machine that you are using. One of the best ways to mine is to go to what is called a cloud-mining contract and purchase it. This agreement will enable you to mine Ether on the Ethereum system. It is recommended that you use Genesis Mining and you can find out more information on them by going to their website.

3. Look at the balance in your wallet and send Ether. When you want to look at your wallet's balance, you will click on "view wallet details," and you will be able to see every transaction that has taken place in your wallet. When you want to send Ether, it will be as simple as clicking on "send transaction" and entering the receiver's public key. Now you are ready to invest with Ethereum!

There are other resources that you will have access to online so that you can find how other people have learned how to invest with Ethereum. It can be hard to invest, but if you follow these steps, you will do just fine. If you are still lost in investing with Ethereum, then you will want to ask someone who has been using Ethereum longer so that they can help you differently.

INVESTING

At this point in time, Ethereum is likened to Bitcoin when it was first started in 2009. Buying Ether could make you money because the price will go up and if you are able to catch the price at the right time, then you will be able to sell it at twice the amount that you first bought it at.

Here are a few reasons that you will want to consider purchasing Ether for long-term investments:

• Cryptocurrency stock is believed to be completed through the distribution and trading of stock on the blockchain application. The trading has made massive differences in the financial sector. The reason that crypto stock trade seems to be the future is that stock trading had middlemen that cryptocurrency has been able to eliminate. Peer trading and fees are also going to be cut out of the equation thanks to applications such as Ethereum. Since peer-to-peer training is free, there will be a better margin for those who are trading stock. It is also going to offer a new category for items that can be traded on a decentralized application. In the end, blockchain will be able to grow in shares that no one will be ready for.

• Ethereum's ecosystem will be increasing. The developers will be working on projects that they are excited to release to the public. Some of the projects will be entitled Colony, Augur and Weifund.

• A transaction volume vs. the market cap: How many transactions that occur will depend on how high the price of Ether is since the nodes on the network will be rewarding the validation of transactions. When Ethereum was first released, it started confirming 15,000 transactions a day. It is predicted that the number of transactions happening will continue to rise as the platform continues to evolve and Dapps continue to increase.

Ether's market cap will be worth one hundred and ninety million dollars. But, the amount of Ether that is available will be based on the number of applications that the platform will have for a short period. Whenever you look at the perspective of a market cap, then it will seem high, and there has to be a decline in the future. But, there is speculation about the value of the drivers for the market cap. These drivers will be the fundamental analysis of how much Ether is currently on the platform.

- Inflationary design: The last driver for ether's value drive will be inflationary design. When the creator of Ethereum first started out on his quest; there was a model of inflation for ether. But, the new distribution system for Ether on the network is also going to go up. The background for this made it to where Ether was considered a product that would facilitate transactions that have to be done on the system. Whenever the price of Ether goes up, then the way that the platform performs will be disrupted.

If the price of Ether goes up, then it is not going to be an investment asset anymore which will end up meaning that there will be an adverse effect on Ethereum's future development. When you look at the current policy of how Ether will be distributed, you will realize that what will happen is not clear enough for you to understand. But, there will be signs of inflation that you will see at a low level; there is the possibility that it will vanish altogether.

However, it is uncertain what will happen with the future distribution of Ether and the other drivers will outweigh the potential risk.

TRADING

Once you have obtained some Ether, you will be able to transfer them to an exchange so that you can begin trading. The process for moving your cryptocurrency to an exchange will vary depending on the exchange that you are using. For example, if you are using Poloniex you are no longer going to be able to register and make trades if you are living in New York. This policy was put in place because of various regulations that Poloniex thinks are too expensive to deal with.

Therefore, once you have gotten Ether, you will want to use Kraken. Kraken is one of the highest ranked exchanges and has a good reputation, not to mention it is one of the first exchanges that started trading Ether.

The first step will be to open an account. Opening an account will be similar to any other site that you have opened an account on; you will use your email and create a password to get into the account. Next, you will need to go through all of their compliance steps, which are typical steps that will be taken in verifying your address. There are various levels of registration depending on the information that is provided by you. The first two levels will be the levels that allow you to trade and pull out a decent amount of cryptocurrency and all you will need to input is your address and your phone number. However, if you want to trade on a larger scale, you will be required to register your passport and a utility bill to prove your address.

After you have gotten through all the levels of verification so that you can complete trades, then you will deposit Ether or fiat currency. Thankfully Kraken provides instructions on how to deposit money into your account. Making any sort of deposit will generate an address that your funds will be sent from. You will then need to create a transaction. After that has been done, Ethereum will appear in your account after a short amount of time.

Once your transaction has been confirmed and the sufficient amount of time has passed, you will be allowed to start trading. To work out the best price, you will want to use a combination of the trading platforms to look at prices across the board to ensure that you are not paying a higher fee than someone else would on a different website.

CHAPTER FOUR:
UNDERSTANDING ETHEREUM

Cryptocurrency has been creating quite a storm in the digital market and Bitcoin is the most popular crypto coin, which has become familiar to most of the crypto enthusiasts. When the price value of Bitcoin surged to new heights in November 2017, the whole world did turn to notice this well-known crypto coin that was trying to change the meaning of trading in the financial world.

People started scrutinizing the cryptocurrency market and were excited to know that more crypto coins were available in the digital market. Bitcoin, which is referred to as the 'virtual gold' served as an inspiration to Vitalik Buterin – the founder of 'Ethereum.' He referred Ethereum to be the silver to Bitcoin's gold. But there was a major difference between Bitcoin and Ethereum. Bitcoin is a cryptocurrency, but Ethereum is NOT a cryptocurrency. Ethereum was developed as an open source platform, which helped to build new, decentralized applications based on the user's requirement.

Does that mean Ethereum cannot be used a cryptocurrency? Ethereum is much more than a cryptocurrency. The decentralized apps, which are developed in Ethereum platform, are known as 'Dapps,' and these Dapps operate in a peer-to-peer network model. It follows the blockchain model similar to that of Bitcoin. The thing that makes Ethereum more advanced compared to Bitcoin is – the 'smart contract.' The blockchain technology used in Bitcoin is specific only to cryptocurrencies and doesn't serve any other purpose, but it is not the same with Ethereum platform.

The blockchain technology in Ethereum's platform has much more uses than that of cryptocurrency. The 'smart contract' is a protocol, which needs to be written by the developers who are developing applications to run on the Ethereum platform. The smart contract has a set of rules or procedures on how a transaction needs to be handled. The small contract can store data or information, work together with other contracts and execute logic (as written by the developer).

This can be compared to the regular legal agreement which is utilized in almost all the fields for executing specific tasks, such as registering a house, getting an asset registered, etc. Smart contracts are used in places where 'permanent records' are required, and developers write these contracts accordingly.

ETHER – THE CRYPTOCURRENCY

Ether or ETH is the crypto token, which is used as 'payments' for transactions that happen on the Ethereum platform. Is it confusing? When someone running a node (participant in the network) processes your program's transaction using an application written on the Ethereum platform, he or she gets paid in Ether (the cryptocurrency of Ethereum) for the same.

Ether is the incentive paid to the developers to develop quality applications in Ethereum platform.

Ether is the digital oil for the Ethereum platform to run on! Ether can be bought just like Bitcoin using cryptocurrency exchanges. Mining ether is a bit different than mining Bitcoin. Ethereum platform users get dual benefits in its mining process:

- Generating new crypto coin – Ether

- Providing incentive to the people for maintaining a strong Ethereum blockchain by encouraging more people to join the network.

Around 94 million ethers (ETH) are generated when every 15 seconds a miner wins his reward. As more people and businesses are trying to use the Ethereum network to build applications satisfying their requirements, they have started to buy and hold 'Ether' as the crypto-coin, required to pay for the network's computing power.

Why would anyone want to use Ethereum network?

The founder of Ethereum was a big fan of Bitcoin, and he had developed this new platform "Ethereum" with the intent of building a system that would make it possible to handle more complex financial transactions and program these transactions according to user's requirements. The blockchain used in Ethereum platform is referred to as Ethereum blockchain, and it is completely independent of the Bitcoin's blockchain.

Let us look at an example to understand why an Ethereum platform would be necessary. When two companies would like to collaborate to carry out a complex financial transaction such as settling a stock option, they would most likely go to a third party (stock exchange) to perform the transaction as the two companies don't trust each other. Now, this process would cost them two things:

- Trusting a third party

- Paying a hefty amount as service charge to the third party

This is where Ethereum platform comes into the picture – when both the companies use Ethereum; they can perform the stock transactions on a shared system allowing them to check records simultaneously and both these companies would also be saving on the 'service charge.' How does this happen? Smart contracts can be written based on the requirements of these two companies, as in, how they want the stock to be distributed, the price value charges, etc. This smart contract can then be executed on the 'Dapp' application developed in the Ethereum platform thereby satisfying the users' needs.

Ethereum has been proved to provide solutions to loads of complex financial transactions that usually happen in financial companies (which don't trust any of their competitors). Banks and financial institutions are looking at Ethereum as a central operating system for most of the trading markets by replacing the intermediaries and exchanges with Ethereum network.

Quorum is the private version of Ethereum created by J P Morgan Chase for their trading markets. There are many more companies who have tried experimenting with Ethereum. Toyota and Samsung are using this platform to keep track of products moving through supply chains involving many players. The group 'Enterprise Ethereum Alliance' is bringing together more companies and enterprises to work on developing applications in Ethereum platform, which can be used specifically as per the need (corporate setting); some others are developing their versions of the Ethereum platform. Though companies are trying to build their private network, there are high chances that they might get clubbed to the public Ethereum network.

MICROSOFT AND ETHEREUM

Microsoft was one of the biggest tech giants who took Bitcoin seriously in 2015 and declared Bitcoin as one of their payment networks to make purchases on Microsoft online store. Microsoft went a step further with Ethereum as a platform and designed a similar framework – Coco.

Microsoft designed the Coco framework to help enterprises and businesses to configure and deploy a blockchain network swiftly and effortlessly. It was designed as 'blockchain as a service' (BaaS), the Azure blockchain service (cloud) and to facilitate blockchain implementation by adjusting to the existing blockchain protocols or creating a new blockchain protocol from scratch.

The Coco framework offered the following benefits:

- It had the capacity to process over 1600 transactions per second (this was more than what Bitcoin and Ethereum blockchain could offer at that time)

- It enabled many to develop their own private blockchain.

- Trusted Execution Environment (TEE) was the unique technology used to host the blockchain code in a secure box, which uses Windows Virtual Secure Mode or Intel's Software Guard Extensions to validate the environment.

The high-level overview of the coco system had the following (bottom to top):

- TEE (Windows VSM, Intel SGX) – first layer

- Coco framework – second layer
- Blockchain (Ethereum or another private blockchain such as Quorom, Corda, HyperLedger Sawtooth, etc.) – third layer
- Decentralized applications (Dapp) – fourth layer

Though the Coco framework works with many private blockchain, Ethereum was the popularly used platform by many enterprises.

COMPARISON BETWEEN ETHEREUM AND BITCOIN

Ethereum and Bitcoin are similar to DOS and Windows; when the computer was first introduced to the world, the first operating system DOS was the crucial part of the computer revolution. Only technical geeks used computers when DOS was the operating system, but when Mac OS and Windows came into the market, the computer became a household property. Computers became an essential commodity like television and other household gadgets. What was the reason? DOS was complicated and tricky. Only experts who could understand programming codes could use them, as very few applications ran on the OS and it was so hard to learn. On the other hand, with Mac OS and windows, the applications that were built on them were user-friendly and easy to use. The graphical user interface (GUI) of these operating systems (both Windows and Mac OS) was easy to learn and quick to understand.

Bitcoin is the DOS here which is pretty complicated to learn and tricky to use as an application whereas Ethereum is like the Mac OS or windows which provides features for the developers to create new applications and use the existing applications with minor changes in the blockchain technology. 2017 is the new 2000 (internet boom) for the cryptocurrency and blockchain technology. More companies are coming up with innovative ideas and creative business models in the blockchain technology.

We cannot deny the fact that Bitcoin is currently charging high transaction fees which are pushing many crypto enthusiasts to look at other cryptocurrencies in the crypto market.

The Ethereum developer conference – DevCon3 witnessed close to 2000 developers who were ready to push the boundaries of blockchain innovation thereby securing Ethereum's future.

Conclusion

Ethereum is a vast field, and it's developing itself every day to include more and more things. The future of Ethereum is bright as people are getting aware of it and companies and startups have started to grow around it.

There can be many reasons for you to use Ethereum – from mining to making decentralized applications that perform complex functions. If you do want to start mining, you should look at the possible problems that you might run into and the costs associated with it.

Ethereum requires not just your time, but also your money; from a security point of view Ethereum is relatively safe, but that doesn't mean you can't make a bad investment. It's important to look at all of your options before you invest in Ethereum.

Most importantly, know what you're getting into and how to do things within the network. Knowledge of the network is essential is making a sound investment decision.

Sources

- http://america.aljazeera.com/articles/2014/4/7/code-your-own-utopiameetethereumbitcoinasmostambitioussuccessor.html
- https://blog.ethereum.org/2015/03/03/ethereum-launch-process/
- https://web.archive.org/web/20140302035654/http://blog.ethereum.org/2014/01/23/ethereum-now-going-public/
- https://www.coindesk.com/information/will-ethereum-scale/
- https://www.coindesk.com/ethereum-casper-proof-stake-rewrite-rules-blockchain/
- http://ethdocs.org/en/latest/introduction/what-is-ethereum.html#ethereum-virtual-machine
- https://www.nytimes.com/2017/10/01/technology/what-is-Ethereum.html
- https://www.bbntimes.com/en/technology/understanding-Ethereum
- https://www.coindesk.com/2017-bitcoins-year-2018-will-Ethereums/

Thank you for reading this book. Please leave an honest review at

https://www.amazon.com/dp/B078L7CFXX

Thank you!

www.ingramcontent.com/pod-product-compliance
Lightning Source LLC
Chambersburg PA
CBHW030058230526
45471CB00003B/1147